SCIENCE WORKS

THE ROCK FACTORY

THE STORY ABOUT THE ROCK CYCLE

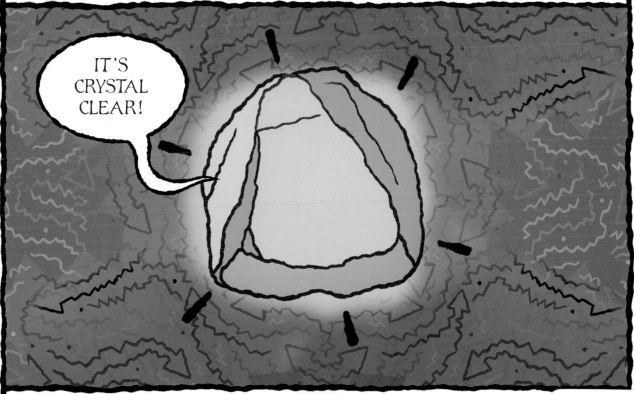

IT'S CRYSTAL CLEAR!

Jacqui Bailey Matthew Lilly

Picture Window Books • Minneapolis, Minnesota

Editor: Jacqueline A. Wolfe
Page Production: Brandie E. Shoemaker
Creative Director: Keith Griffin
Editorial Director: Carol Jones

First American edition published in 2006 by
Picture Window Books
5115 Excelsior Boulevard
Suite 232
Minneapolis, MN 55416
1-877-845-8392
www.picturewindowbooks.com

First published in Great Britain by
A & C Black Publishers Limited
37 Soho Square, London W1D 3QZ

Printed in the United States of America.

Library of Congress Cataloging-in-Publication Data
Bailey, Jacqui.
The rock factory : a story about the rock cycle / by Jacqui Bailey ; illustrated by Matthew Lilly.
p. cm. — (Science works)
Includes bibliographical references and index.
ISBN 1-4048-1596-1
1. Petrology—Juvenile literature. 2. Geochemical cycles—Juvenile literature. I. Lilly, Matthew, ill. II. Title.
QE432.2.B348 2006
552—dc22   2005030011

For Louis
JB

For Phil and Alex
ML

Special thanks to our advisers for their expertise, research, and advice:

Dr. Robin Armstrong, Peter Tandy, and Charlotte Stockley
Mineralogy Department at the Natural History Museum
London, England

Larry M. Browning, Ph.D., Professor,
Physics Department South Dakota State University,
Brookings, South Dakota, USA

Susan Kesselring, M.A., Literacy Educator
Rosemount—Apple Valley—Eagan (Minnesota) School District

Our story of
a stone begins
thousands of
millions of
years ago.

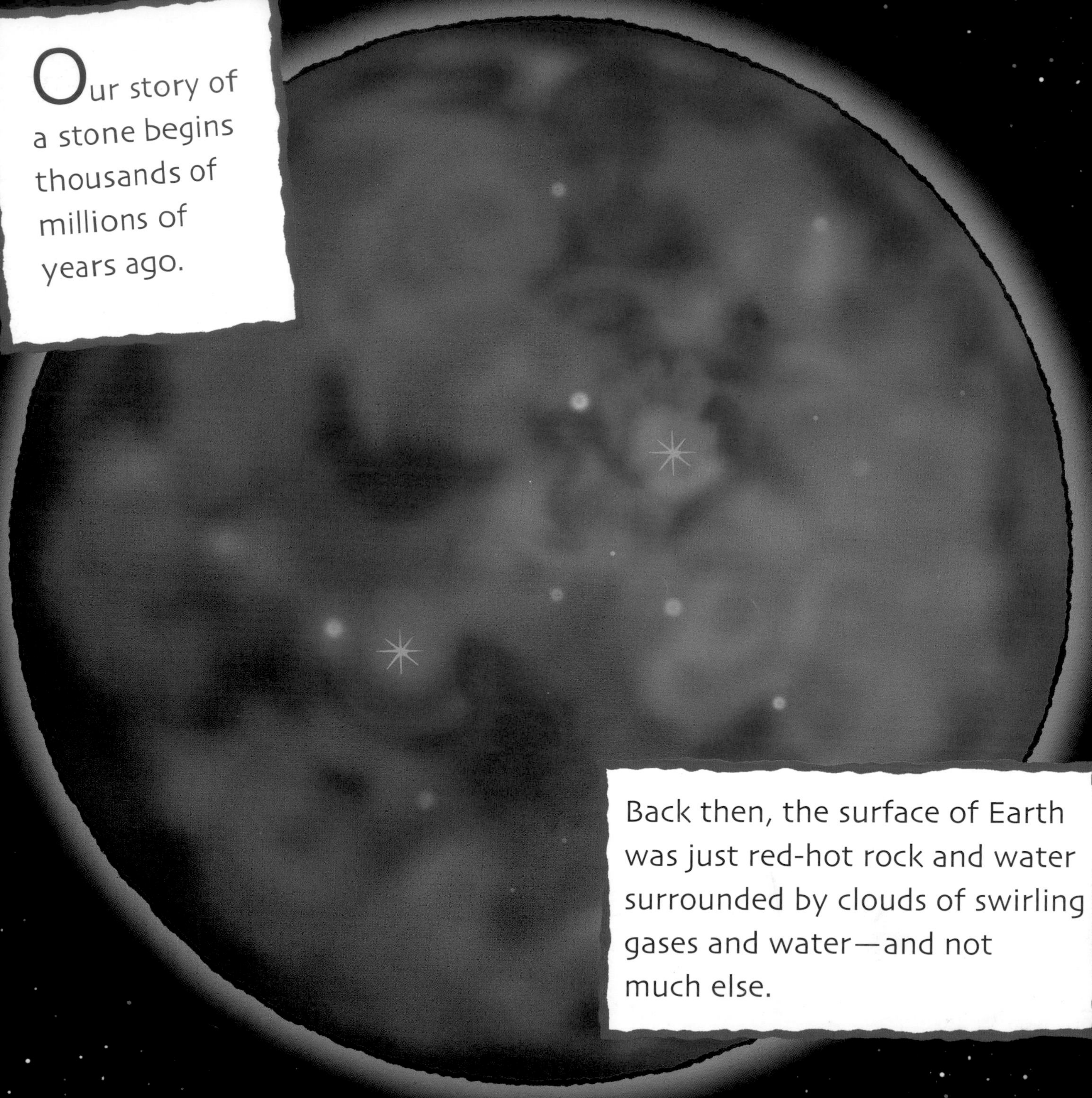

Back then, the surface of Earth
was just red-hot rock and water
surrounded by clouds of swirling
gases and water—and not
much else.

There were no plants or animals. The only things that moved were the wind, water, and rivers of hot rock from exploding volcanoes.

The rivers of rock were escaping from the rock factory deep inside Earth.

Our planet is mostly made of rock, but it isn't solid all the way through. It's made up of different layers like a soft-boiled egg.

The top layer is the crust. This thin layer of hard rock is like the shell of an egg. The crust covers all of Earth. The land we live on is part of it, and the oceans fill the low parts of the crust.

HMMM, I'M FEELING A LITTLE CRUSTY TODAY!

Underneath the crust is the mantle. This is a very thick layer of immensely hot and heavy rock material—like a thick, stiff cake mix.

The mantle is the rock factory. It's where most of the rock in the crust originally came from, and it's where the stone in our story was made.

Below the mantle is the super-hot core. It has a layer of liquid metal on the outside and is solid metal on the inside. The core is like an oven at the heart of Earth, and its heat spreads right up through the mantle.

The mantle is hottest next to the core and grows gradually cooler as it gets closer and closer to the crust.

Billions of years ago, the clump of material that would make our stone was gradually working its way up through the mantle.

8

As the material crept upward, the heat around it grew a little less intense. The weight pressing down from above began to lighten.

ARE WE THERE YET?

HEY! IT'S GETTING COOLER!

Eventually it arrived at a special spot, and it began to change ...

Crust

Mantle

Core

Rock making is a very slow business. It takes millions and millions of years for rock material to rise from the bottom of the mantle to the top.

Our clump of material had reached just the right place in the mantle for it to turn into a stone.

Most minerals turn into crystals, but only when the pressure (caused by the weight of the rocks above them) and the temperature (level of heat) are exactly right for that type of mineral.

How does that happen?
Well, it goes something like this.

Rock is made from stuff called minerals. There are lots of different kinds of minerals and they all shift and stir around in the mantle like the ingredients in a cake mix.

HEY!
WHAT'S
HAPPENING?

HELP!

As minerals get closer to the crust, they begin to cool. As they cool, they harden into special flat-sided shapes called crystals.

Each kind of mineral forms its own type of crystal—and when lots of crystals lock together, they make rocks.

Crystals

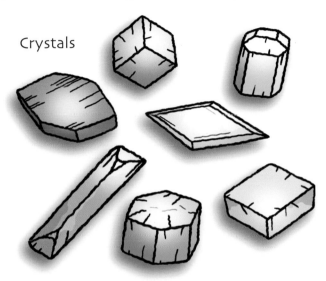

Most rocks and stones are made of a mixture of minerals with crystals of different shapes and sizes.

Granite is a hard, speckled-looking rock made of four kinds of crystals. Each speckle is a different crystal.

Crystals

Granite

HEAR THAT? I'M A SPECIAL STONE.

But our stone was different—its crystals were all the same. They had formed from just one material called carbon. This made our stone a very special stone.

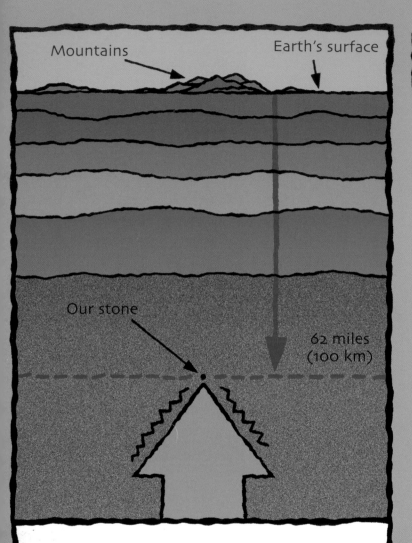

Mountains

Earth's surface

Our stone

62 miles
(100 km)

Millions more years passed and our stone moved higher up the mantle. It was now about 62 miles (100 kilometers) below the surface.

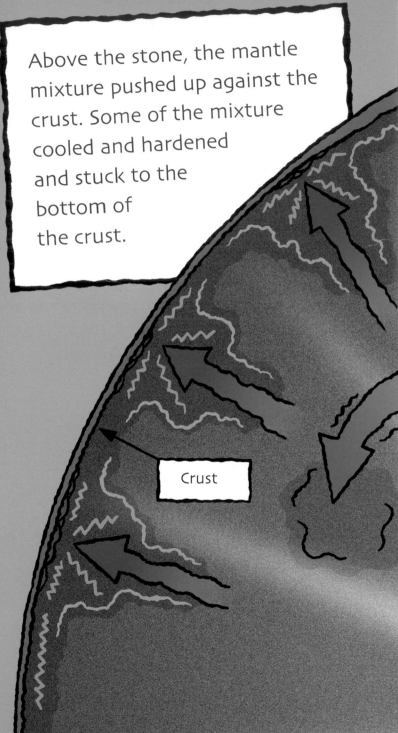

Above the stone, the mantle mixture pushed up against the crust. Some of the mixture cooled and hardened and stuck to the bottom of the crust.

Crust

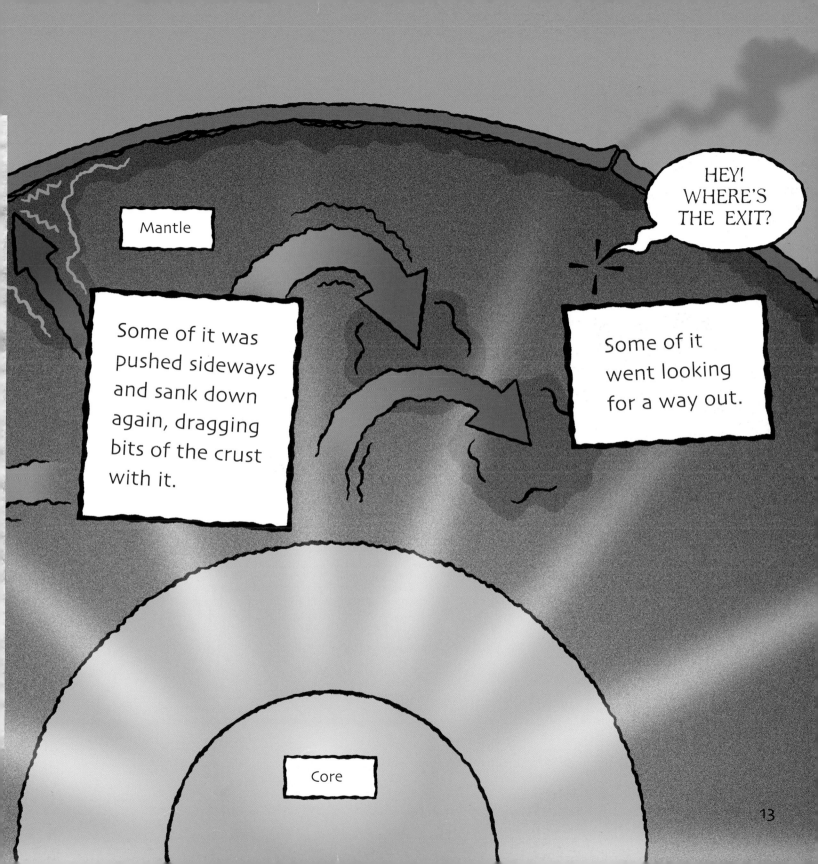

As the rock mixture moves up the mantle, some of it softens and turns into a grainy liquid. This liquid is called magma.

If it finds a gap, it surges into it, tearing a hole right through the crust and gushing onto the surface, like soda pop from a shaken bottle.

Magma moves more easily through the mantle than the rest of the rock mixture. When it reaches the crust it builds up underneath it. Then it pushes and squeezes its way into any gaps in the crust that it can find.

This is what happens in a volcano.

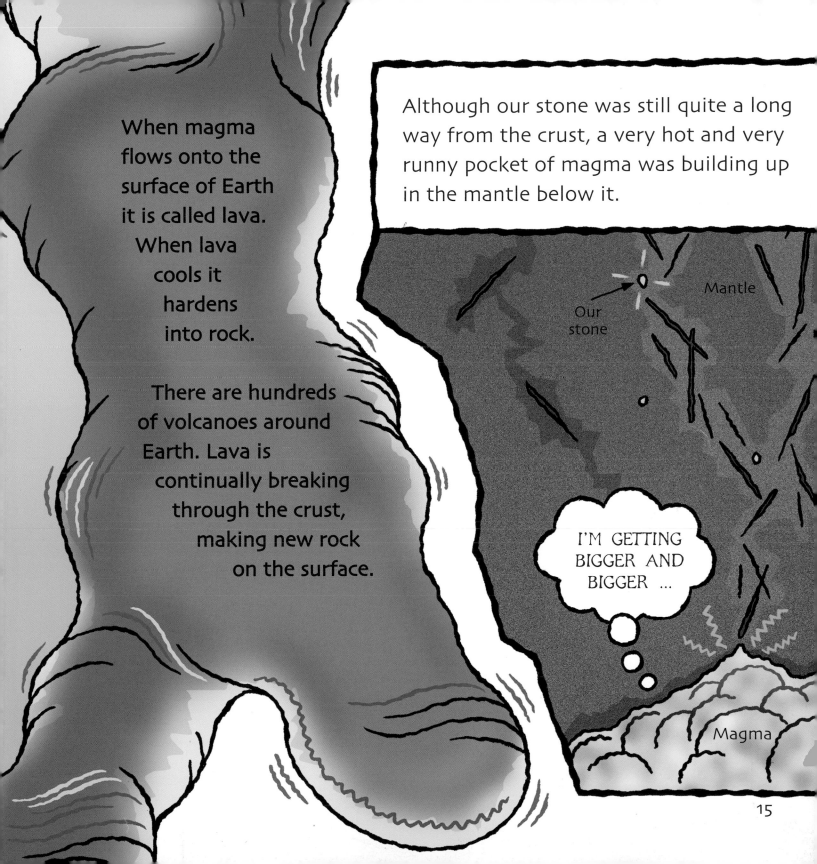

When magma flows onto the surface of Earth it is called lava. When lava cools it hardens into rock.

There are hundreds of volcanoes around Earth. Lava is continually breaking through the crust, making new rock on the surface.

Although our stone was still quite a long way from the crust, a very hot and very runny pocket of magma was building up in the mantle below it.

Mantle

Our stone

I'M GETTING BIGGER AND BIGGER ...

Magma

The pocket of magma got bigger and bigger and, instead of seeping through the mantle mixture like most magma, it pushed and pushed against it.

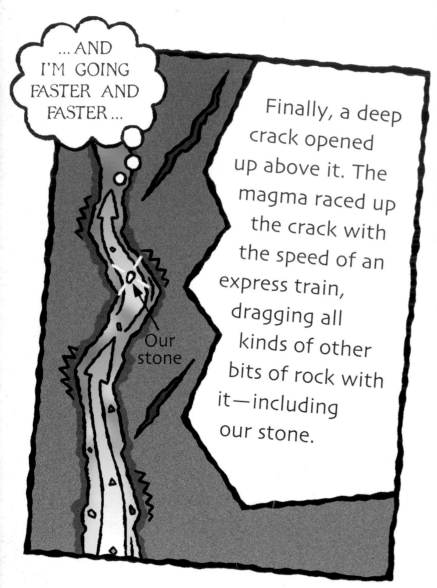

Finally, a deep crack opened up above it. The magma raced up the crack with the speed of an express train, dragging all kinds of other bits of rock with it—including our stone.

Our stone

In just a few hours, our stone traveled farther than it had in millions of years. It was carried out of the mantle and into the crust.

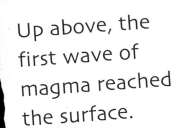

Up above, the first wave of magma reached the surface.

The ground ripped open and a blast of scorching steam and ash exploded into the air, instantly burning up anything it touched.

... EXPLODE!

Lumps of red-hot rock and blobs of lava rained down around the volcano like a gigantic firework, and our stone was brought closer and closer to the surface.

Not many volcanoes are as explosive as this. With some, lava oozes out of the crust slowly like jelly squeezed from a doughnut.

When the explosion ended, there was a huge hole in the ground. It looked like a giant ice-cream cone filled with shattered rocks and cooling magma. The stone stayed where it was.

Time passed and on the surface things changed. The bowl-shaped top of the volcano filled with water and made a lake.

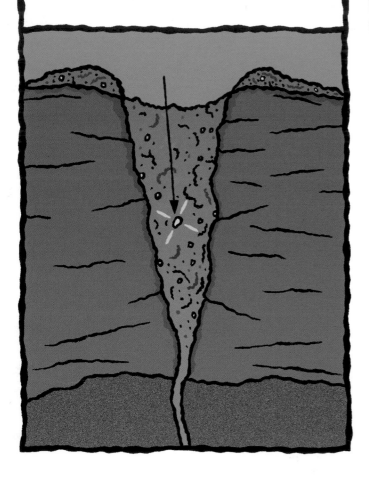

Birds and other animals came to drink at the lake, and trees and bushes grew around it.

The wind and weather wore away at the bowl. The lake overflowed and ran down the hillside to join a river far below.

Over millions of years, the ground around the bowl and the rock inside it were broken up into tiny pieces and washed away.

One day, our stone was washed away, too. It rolled downhill and into the river.

The stone sat with other stones on the riverbed. Fish nosed around it and sometimes layers of mud covered it.

When animals waded into the water they churned the riverbed around. The stone was rolled from place to place.

One day, a boy came and played by the river. He dug his hands into the riverbed and pulled up a handful of wet, shiny pebbles.

He picked out our stone and looked at it carefully. It wasn't like the other stones. It was muddy and dull but it looked like a piece of glass. He could almost see through it.

MAYBE THIS IS A LUCKY STONE. I THINK I'LL KEEP IT.

The boy put the stone in his pocket and took it home.

When the boy showed the stone to his parents they got very excited. They took it to a jeweler's shop in a nearby town.

The jeweler held the stone up to the light and peered at it closely through his magnifying glass.

He reached for some tools and tried to scratch the surface of the stone, but he couldn't mark it. Then he measured it, weighed it, and wrote down some notes.

At last, he looked up. "You're a very lucky boy," he said.

MORE GREAT STUFF TO KNOW

DIAMONDS ARE FOREVER

Diamonds are the hardest natural material in the world. They can only be cut by another diamond.

> LOOK OUT, EARTH, HERE I COME!

Diamonds are also among the oldest things on Earth. They may be 3 billion years old! But some diamonds are even older than this. They are found in meteorites—chunks of rock that fall to Earth from space. Meteorites can contain tiny bits of diamond up to 5 billion years old.

> PHEW!

A COOL CRUST

Scientists think Earth formed from dust and gas whirling around the sun about 4.6 billion years ago. It took more than a billion years for Earth to cool down enough for the crust to form and the oceans to fill with water. The crust is much thinner under the oceans than under the land. In some places it is only about 5 miles (6 km) thick. Under land it can be up to 43.5 miles (70 km) thick.

Hot Rocks

granite

Most rocks belong to one of three groups. Rocks that are made when magma or lava hardens are called igneous (*ig-nee-us*) or fiery rock. Granite is a type of igneous rock.

Rocks that are heated or squeezed so much they turn into a different sort of rock are called metamorphic (*met-uh-mor-fik*) or changed rock. Marble is a metamorphic rock made from limestone.

marble

Limestone belongs to the third group, known as sedimentary (*se-da-men-ta-ree*) rock. When surface rocks are worn down into tiny pieces and washed into the ocean, they form layers of mud on the ocean floor. Over millions of years the layers pile up, until the ones at the bottom are squeezed into solid rock again.

Mighty Minerals

Minerals don't only make rocks, they help build our bodies, too. Some of the chemicals in minerals, such as calcium, help our bones and teeth to grow properly. We get most of the minerals we need from the food we eat. Farmers often add extra minerals to the soil to grow stronger and healthier plants.

TRY IT AND SEE

GROW YOUR OWN CRYSTALS

Lots of everyday materials are made from crystals. Water forms crystals when it freezes into ice. Snowflakes are tiny masses of ice crystals. Salt crystals form when seawater dries up.

Try growing your own crystals. It may take a week or so, The longer you wait, the better the crystals will be.

You will need:
- A measuring cup
- Hot water
- Salt
- A teaspoon
- A wooden spoon
- Food dye (if you have it)
- A glass jar
- A pencil and some yarn

1 Ask an adult to boil some water and pour about 1/2 cup (100 ml) into the measuring cup.

2 While the water is still hot, add a teaspoon of salt and carefully stir the mixture with the wooden spoon. When the salt has dissolved, add another teaspoonful.

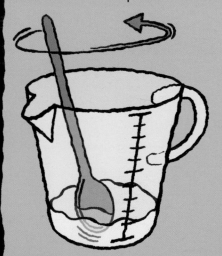

When that has dissolved, add another one. Keep going until the salt stops dissolving and starts to collect in the bottom of the cup—after about 4 teaspoons.

3 Stir in a few drops of food dye. This isn't vital, but your crystals will look more interesting.

4 Pour the colored saltwater into the glass jar.

5 Cut a short length of yarn and tie one end to the middle of the pencil. Balance the pencil on top of the jar so that the yarn dangles into the liquid.

6 Put your jar somewhere where it will not be disturbed. Gradually, the water in the jar will cool down and start to evaporate. It will turn to a gas and float into the air.

The remaining water will not be able to hold onto the dissolved salt any longer. The salt will cling to the yarn and to the sides of the jar and form crystals.

Once crystals start forming on the yarn, try putting it into a fresh batch of salt water (make sure the mixture has cooled first). This encourages the crystals to grow on the yarn rather than on the sides of the jar.

ROCKY FACTS

Diamond mining in South Africa began in the 1860s when a 15-year-old boy, Erasmus Jacobs, found "a pebble" on the bank of a river on his father's farm. It was a large diamond. Today, most of the world's diamonds come from mines in Australia, Africa, Russia, and Canada.

The deepest hole ever drilled into Earth was in Russia. It reached just over 7.5 miles (12 km) down into the crust. After that, the heat and pressure of the rock softened the metal drill so much it could not go any further.

There are about 500 active volcanoes in the world today and lots more that are sleeping or dormant. Volcanoes can be dormant for thousands of years and then suddenly burst into life again.

GLOSSARY

core—the inner layer of Earth

crust—the outer layer of Earth

igneous rock—rock made when hot melted rock cools down

lava—liquid rock that flows out of a volcano and hardens as it cools

limestone—hard rock that contains calcium

magma—hot, melted rock beneath Earth's surface

mantle—the middle layer of Earth

metamorphic rock—rock formed by heat and pressure

minerals—the materials that make up a rock

volcano—mountains that emit hot gases and melted rock from deep within Earth

ON THE WEB

FactHound offers a safe, fun way to find Internet sites related to this book. All of the sites on FactHound have been researched by our staff.

1. Visit *www.facthound.com*

2. Type in this special code for age-appropriate sites: 1404815961

3. Click on the FETCH IT button.

   Your trusty FactHound will fetch the best sites for you!

INDEX

Read all of the books in the Science Works series:

A Drop in the Ocean
The Story of Water
1-4048-0566-4

Charged Up
The Story of Electricity
1-4048-0568-0

Cracking Up
A Story About Erosion
1-4048-1594-5

Monster Bones
The Story of a Dinosaur Fossil
1-4048-0565-6

The Rock Factory
A Story of Rocks and Stones
1-4048-1596-1

Staying Alive
The Story of a Food Chain
1-4048-1595-3

Sun Up, Sun Down
The Story of Day and Night
1-4048-0567-2

Up, Down, All Around
A Story of Gravity
1-4048-1597-X

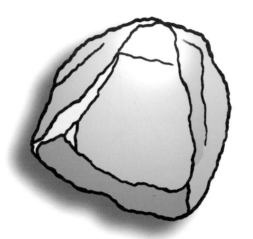